AF469139

POSITIVELY POOH

A Book for Bothersome Days

EGMONT

We bring stories to life

First published in Great Britain 2005 by Egmont UK Limited
239 Kensington High Street, London W8 6SA

ISBN 978 1 4052 2046 0
ISBN 1 4052 2046 5

3 5 7 9 10 8 6 4 2

A CIP catalogue record for this title is available from the British Library

Printed and bound in Malaysia

POSITIVELY POOH

A Book for Bothersome Days

A.A. Milne
Illustrated by E.H. Shepard

EGMONT

Flowers brighten up even the most bothersome of days

Piglet had got up early that morning to pick himself a bunch of violets; and when he had picked them and put them in a pot in the middle of his house, it suddenly came over him that nobody had ever picked Eeyore a bunch of violets, and the more he thought of this, the more he thought how sad it was to be an Animal who had never had a bunch of violets picked for him. So he hurried out again, saying to himself, 'Eeyore, Violets,' and then 'Violets, Eeyore,' in case he forgot, because it was that sort of day . . .

Delegate on those busy days

It was going to be one of Rabbit's busy days. As soon as he woke up he felt important, as if everything depended upon him. It was just the day for Organizing Something, or for Writing a Notice Signed Rabbit, or for Seeing What Everybody Else Thought About It.

Stop to pass the time of day

'I make it seventeen days come Friday since anybody spoke to me.'
'It certainly isn't seventeen days –'
'Come Friday,' explained Eeyore.
'And to-day's Saturday,' said Rabbit. 'So that would make it eleven days. And I was here myself a week ago.'
'Not conversing,' said Eeyore. 'Not first one and then the other. You said "Hallo" and Flashed Past. I saw your tail a hundred yards up the hill as I was meditating my reply. I *had* thought of saying "What?" – but of, course, it was then too late.'
'Well, I was in a hurry.'

'When you wake up in the morning, Pooh,'
said Piglet at last, 'what's the first thing you
say to yourself?'
'What's for breakfast?' said Pooh. 'What do
you say, Piglet?'
'I say, I wonder what's going to happen exciting
to-day?' said Piglet.
Pooh nodded thoughtfully.
'It's the same thing,' he said.

Think about all the exciting things that are going to happen to-day (particularly on Monday mornings)

Things can only get better, especially if you have just lost your tail

'Good morning, Eeyore,' said Pooh.
'Good morning, Pooh Bear,' said Eeyore gloomily. 'If it *is* a good morning,' he said. 'Which I doubt,' said he.

Try to maintain your sunny outlook

'Hallo, Eeyore,' said Christopher Robin, as he opened the door and came out. 'How are *you*?'

'It's snowing still,' said Eeyore gloomily.

'So it is.'

'*And* freezing.'

'Is it?'

'Yes,' said Eeyore. 'However,' he said, brightening up a little, 'we haven't had an earthquake lately.'

Taking a break restores your energy levels

Christopher Robin called 'Halt!' and they all sat down and rested.

'I think,' said Christopher Robin, 'that we ought to eat all our Provisions now, so that we shan't have so much to carry.'

'Eat all our what?' said Pooh.

'All that we've brought,' said Piglet, getting to work.

That's a good idea,' said Pooh, and he got to work too.

Recognise when it's time to take a holiday

'And how are you?' said Winnie-the-Pooh.
Eeyore shook his head from side to side.
'Not very how,' he said. 'I don't seem to have felt at all how for a long time.'
'Dear, dear,' said Pooh, 'I'm sorry about that. Let's have a look at you.'

Know when it's time for a new start

Pooh had wandered into the Hundred Acre Wood, and was standing in front of what had once been Owl's House. It didn't look at all like a house now; it looked like a tree which had been blown down; and as soon as a house looks like that, it is time you tried to find another one.

. . . when you are a Bear of Very Little Brain, and you Think of Things, you find sometimes that a Thing which seemed very Thingish inside you is quite different when it gets out into the open and has other people looking at it.

It helps to air your ideas

It's the thought that counts

'I've brought you a little present,' said Pooh excitedly.
'I've had it,' said Eeyore.
Pooh had now splashed across the stream to Eeyore, and Piglet was sitting a little way off, his head in his paws, snuffling to himself.
'It's a Useful Pot,' said Pooh. 'Here it is. And it's got "A Very Happy Birthday with love from Pooh" written on it. That's what all that writing is. And it's for putting things in. There!'
When Eeyore saw the pot, he became quite excited.
'Why!' he said. 'I believe my Balloon will just go into that Pot!'

Although accidents will happen, you can limit the risks

Eeyore whispered back: 'I'm not saying there won't be an Accident now, mind you. They're funny things, Accidents. You never have them till you're having them.'

Avoid people who will make you miserable

'It's bad enough,' said Eeyore, almost breaking down, 'being miserable myself, what with no presents and no cake and no candles, and no proper notice taken of me at all, but if everybody else is going to be miserable too –'

'I have been Foolish and Deluded,' said he, 'and I am a Bear of No Brain at All.'

'You're the Best Bear in All the World,' said Christopher Robin soothingly.

'Am I?' said Pooh hopefully. And then he brightened up suddenly.

You are not as stupid as you think

Prevent complete exhaustion with a Pooh power nap

Pooh was so tired when he got home that, in the very middle of his supper, after he had been eating for little more than half-an-hour, he fell fast asleep in his chair, and slept and slept and slept.

Look the part so you'll feel Ready for Anything

As soon as he saw the Big Boots, Pooh knew that an Adventure was going to happen, and he brushed the honey off his nose with the back of his paw, and spruced himself up as well as he could, so as to look Ready for Anything.

It's always wise to apologise

'Oh!' said Pooh, and scrambled up as quickly as he could. 'Did I fall on you, Piglet?'

'You fell on me,' said Piglet, feeling himself all over.

'I didn't mean to,' said Pooh sorrowfully.

'I didn't mean to be underneath,' said Piglet sadly. 'But I'm all right now, Pooh, and I *am* so glad it was you.'

Don't be afraid to ask others for help

At last he found a pencil and a small piece of dry paper, and a bottle with a cork to it. And he wrote on one side of the paper:

HELP!
PIGLIT (ME)

and on the other side:

IT'S ME PIGLIT, HELP HELP!

Learn to make decisions quickly

'Christopher – *ow*! – Robin,' called out the cloud.

'Yes?'

'I have just been thinking, and I have come to a very important decision. *These are the wrong sort of bees.*'

'Are they?'

'Quite the wrong sort. So I should think they would make the wrong sort of honey, shouldn't you?'

'Would they?'

'Yes. So I think I shall come down.'

'I'm not asking anybody,' said Eeyore. 'I'm just telling everybody. We can look for the North Pole, or we can play "Here we go gathering Nuts and May" with the end part of an ants' nest. It's all the same to me.'

Consider your options carefully

Prioritise on those bothering sorts of days

ORDER OF LOOKING FOR THINGS.

1. Special Place. (*To find Piglet.*)
2. Piglet. (*To find who Small is.*)
3. Small. (*To find Small.*)
4. Rabbit (*To tell him I've found Small.*)
5. Small Again. (*To tell him I've found Rabbit.*)

'It's a funny thing about Tiggers,' whispered Tigger to Roo, 'how Tiggers *never* get lost.'

'Why don't they, Tigger?'

'They just don't,' explained Tigger. 'That's how it is.'

Check you are you going in the right direction

Too many social engagements can prove bothersome

'I might have known,' said Eeyore. 'After all, one can't complain. I have my friends. Somebody spoke to me only yesterday. And was it last week or the week before that Rabbit bumped into me and said "Bother!" The Social Round. Always something going on.'

'What do I look like?'

'You look like a bear holding on to a balloon,' you said

'Not,' said Pooh anxiously, '– not like a small black cloud in a blue sky?'

'Not very much.'

'Ah, well, perhaps from up here it looks different. And, as I say, you never can tell with bees.'

Always have a plan Bee

Those with Brain don't always know it all

Owl looked at the notice again. To one of his education the reading of it was easy. 'Gon out, Backson. Bisy, Backson' – just the sort of thing you'd expect to see on a notice.

'It is quite clear what has happened, my dear Rabbit,' he said. 'Christopher Robin has gone out somewhere with Backson. He and Backson are busy together. Have you seen a Backson anywhere about in the Forest lately?'

'I shall do it,' said Pooh, after waiting a little longer, 'by means of a trap. And it must be a Cunning Trap, so you will have to help me, Piglet.' 'Pooh,' said Piglet, feeling quite happy again now, 'I will.' And then he said, 'How shall we do it?' and Pooh said, 'That's just it. How?' And then they sat down together to think it out.

Use your Cunning to solve problems

Tell yourself you know what you're doing

'Hallo!' said Piglet, 'what are you doing?'
'Hunting,' said Pooh.
'Hunting what?'
'Tracking something,' said Winnie-the-Pooh very mysteriously.
'Tracking what?' said Piglet, coming closer.
'That's just what I ask myself. I ask myself, What?'
'What do you think you'll answer?'
'I shall have to wait until I catch up with it,' said Winnie-the-Pooh.

'Bother!' said Pooh. 'It all comes of trying to be kind to Heffalumps.' And he got back into bed. But he couldn't sleep. The more he tried to sleep, the more he couldn't. He tried Counting Sheep, which is sometimes a good way of getting to sleep, and, as that was no good, he tried counting Heffalumps. And that was worse. Because every Heffalump that he counted was making straight for a pot of Pooh's honey, *and eating it all.* For some minutes he lay there miserably, but when the five hundred and eighty-seventh Heffalump was licking its jaws, and saying to itself, 'Very good honey this, I don't know when I've tasted better,' Pooh could bear it no longer. He jumped out of bed, he ran out of the house, and he ran straight to the Six Pine Trees.

Sometimes it's better
to do something

Make a note of important details

As soon as Rabbit was out of sight, Pooh remembered that he had forgotten to ask who Small was, and whether he was the sort of friend-and-relation who settled on one's nose, or the sort who got trodden on by mistake, and as it was Too Late Now, he thought he would begin the Hunt by looking for Piglet, and asking him what they were looking for before he looked for it.

Reduce headaches – find another way

Here is Edward Bear, coming downstairs now, bump, bump, bump, on the back of his head, behind Christopher Robin. It is, as far as he knows, the only way of coming downstairs, but sometimes he feels that there really is another way, if only he could stop bumping for a moment and think of it. And then he feels that perhaps there isn't.